Seattle Sketcher

Gabriel Campanario

The Seattle Times

Published by Pediment Publishing,
a division of The Pediment Group, Inc.
www.pediment.com. Printed in Canada.

Cover sketch and
back cover photo by
Gabriel Campanario

Ballard Centennial Bell Tower houses the bell that hung above Ballard's City
Hall when the neighborhood was an independent city at the turn of the
20th century.

Preface

When you've lived in a city for a while, it's difficult to see things with fresh eyes. I grew up in Barcelona, a magnificent metropolis by all accounts, yet I can't say I ever fully understood or appreciated its character.

Back then I wasn't looking at things the way urban sketchers do. I wasn't slowing down, paying attention to architectural details, how colors change from morning to evening or the expressions of commuters in packed subways.

As a newcomer to Seattle in 2006, however, everything felt new, and I became a compulsive sketcher. I first drew on a little notebook during my bus commute, lunch breaks from work and family excursions around the Puget Sound region.

Later, when my sketches started appearing in The Seattle Times, I felt obliged to step up my game and began drawing on larger sketchbooks and sheets of hot-press watercolor paper. But even if my tools have evolved, the act of sketching on location has remained the same.

I draw on the spot, usually directly with a fountain pen, unless a complex perspective merits blocking outlines in pencil first. I carry a small set of watercolors and waterbrushes to color the sketches on the go, but if time doesn't allow, I color later while the scene is still fresh in my mind. While it's sometimes tempting to snap a photograph for reference, I never do that. The purpose of my sketching is more journalistic than artistic. I aim to record a moment — that's why I date all my sketches—not to create a picture-perfect postcard.

This plain approach to sketching turned out to be transformative for me. I'm reminded by the selection of newspaper columns in this book that my understanding of Seattle and the people who live here keeps increasing with every sketch I make. To draw on Alki Beach on a cold November day isn't just an exercise in artistic endurance — every stroke of the pen seems to peel off a layer of history. You transport yourself back in time to the days the Seattle pioneers landed on that same shoreline.

Whether you already know my work from the pages of The Seattle Times or just happened upon this book, I hope my impressions of Seattle will help you see the city in a new light, and perhaps even inspire you to pick up your own notebook and start to draw.

gabi campanario

Contents

The magic of the Seattle Center Monorail is hidden under its shiny bumpers, where big and small tires guide the trains along the 1.2-mile track.

MONORAIL

Seattle
MONORAIL
Westlake
Station

4:32 p.m
2·13·12

46°

1.52 p.m
2 | 6 | 13

Introduction

In an age in which nearly every phone has a camera and every pocket has a phone, why do sketches still have stopping power? What is it about ink, paper and watercolors that capture our attention — and imagination?

I put those questions to Gabriel Campanario, The Seattle Times' graphic artist better known as the Seattle Sketcher. Gabi has been drawing all his life, but for the last five years has shared that talent with Times readers every Saturday on the pages of the local section and every day on seattletimes.com.

"A sketch," Gabi told me in the soft Spanish accent of his native Barcelona, "has an inherent nostalgic quality. It leaves room for you to fill in the blanks. You can complete the picture with your memories, your feelings.

"People connect to drawings in a different way."

Gabi clearly has connected with Seattle. Thousands of people turned out for an exhibit of his work at the Museum of History & Industry. And each week brings new notes to his desk at The Times from readers thanking him for his artistry and "affectionate profiles" of the people and places we encounter each day.

You'll find many of those places inside this book, which is divided into scenes of historic Seattle, community sketches, hidden places and changing landscapes. The four major sections are punctuated by galleries dedicated to our whimsical public art, our fascination with flying, our love affair with boats and our sports madness.

It's no accident that Gabi is drawing for a newspaper. The art of illustrating printed texts dates back to Johannes Gutenberg, inventor of the first printing press. For nearly 500 years, illustrations were the only way to tell stories visually until they fell out of favor in the 1920s when photos routinely began appearing in newspapers.

Today, many newspapers still employ illustrators. But only The Seattle Times publishes weekly sketches of the Puget Sound region — sketches that require you to slow down, look deeply and see your world in a slightly different way.

I hope Gabi's drawings help you connect — or reconnect — to your memories, your imagination and your wonder about this amazing place we call home.

Kathy Best, Editor
The Seattle Times

A viewpoint on Lake Washington Boulevard offers this view of the Interstate 90 floating bridges connecting Seattle and Mercer Island.

The
Kalakala
1·30·12

Seeking History
in a New City

Seattle may not have Gothic cathedrals or ancient ruins
as do other popular places around the world, but it has
managed to accumulate a number of iconic landmarks
in a relatively short period of time. These are places that
trigger memories for the old-timers and delight
and enlighten newcomers like me.

I endured a two-hour kayak paddle in an industrial waterway in Tacoma to get an up-close look at the derelict Kalakala ferry.

ALKI BEACH

11·6·13

BIRthplace of SEATTLE

Unwelcoming November chill still marks birthplace of Seattle

Sketched Nov. 6, 2013

An austere monument at Alki Avenue Southwest and 63rd Avenue Southwest marks the "birthplace of Seattle," the point along the West Seattle shoreline where a group of pioneers led by Arthur Denny landed 162 years ago this week.

I used to think the Denny Party stumbled upon these lands the same way Columbus happened upon America. But I know better now. Arthur Denny had dispatched his younger brother, David, to scout the area a few months earlier.

That means the 24 men, women and children who came aboard the schooner Exact had something to look forward to. Namely, the cabin David Denny and fellow pioneer Lee Terry were building to welcome them.

On their arrival, however, they found a big disappointment. David had fallen ill, and the cabin was unfinished — in the middle of November. No wonder "the ladys sat down on the loggs and took A Big Cry," as later reported by a member of the party.

Though a major metropolis has blossomed along Elliott Bay since then, it's not difficult to imagine what the pioneers had to go through that Nov. 13 of 1851. Stand for a few minutes on that beach this time of the year and you'll feel the same chill in the air while seagulls fly through the same cloudy skies that greeted the Denny Party.

I think I would have cried too.

SPACE
NEEDLE

BARnicles

11-6-13

54°

original pipes.

gears to otis elevator

not a Disney exhibit

1
23
13

Mind your step!

Downstairs stroll in an earlier Seattle

Sketched Jan. 23, 2013

Tour guide Rose Zeringer turns off the lights and points to a 120-year-old skylight above us: "This is how they lit up the underground before electricity."

The Underground Tour, created by Bill Speidel in 1965, is no staged production. You get to walk through the subterranean sidewalks and building spaces left behind when the city raised the street levels of downtown Seattle during the Great Fire rebuild of the 1890s.

I used to dismiss this Pioneer Square attraction as a tourist trap, but a visit proved me wrong. The experience is both educational and thrilling. Sketching along the dimly lit corridors, I felt like an old-time newspaper artist at work in the years before photography — I actually took the tour twice to pencil enough detail into my drawings to be able to complete them later from memory.

"If people see what history looks like, they'll be more likely to preserve it," said Zeringer. "Bill started this walking tour to save the neighborhood from the wrecking ball."

This is what they
lantern, torches

drug store

1·23·13

soot
Scandinavian drawing

Rose Zeringer
Tour guide

before
electricity
that
was
the only
way to
light tubes

BRanLon
Brand
eeb,Lec
1965,
March 31
1973

3.36
p.m.

BRuce
Lee
NOV 27 1940
July 20 1973

your inspiration
continues to guide
us toward
our personal
liberation

Día de los Lake View

Sketched Oct. 25, 2011

Día de los Muertos on Nov. 2 always triggers childhood memories of visiting the cemetery with my mom. As is customary in Spain, we would bring fresh flowers to my grandpa's niche and pay respect with a moment of silence.

Though I am thousands of miles away now, I decided to observe the day, if only a bit earlier, with a visit to the city's oldest cemetery, Lake View, on Capitol Hill.

Cemetery manager George Nemeth said more than 40,000 people have been buried here since 1872, and they bury an average of 120 more every year. Imagine how many people have a special connection with this hilltop and its magnificent views east and west.

People also visit for the history lesson, as many of Seattle's pioneers are buried here. Of all the famous graves to sketch, I was drawn to Princess Angeline's simple granite rock. The daughter of Chief Seattle, I learned, requested to be buried next to her good friend, Henry Yesler.

HENRY
YESLER →

12
49
P.M.

LAKEView
cemetery

10 25 11

← PRINCESS Angeline, daughter of
Chief Seattle

KERRYPARK

9·7·2012

3·12 p.m.

Space Needle contest should go for the gold

Sketched Sept. 7, 2012

Are you used to Galaxy Gold yet?

That bright orange paint atop the Space Needle has grown on me, so much that now I don't want it to go away. But as the 50th anniversary celebrations come to a close, the Space Needle has plans to replace the gold top with a winning design from entries anyone can submit.

As an artist, you'd think I'd like a creative contest, but the prize seems too small for such a big project. The winner, says the Needle's campaign, will get "bragging rights … 50th anniversary mementos and MORE really cool stuff!"

At any rate, why mess with success? I think Galaxy Gold has many fans, if only based on my informal poll at Kerry Park.

"It's nice they went back to the original color," said Brittany Nicole, a photographer from Texas. Tour guide Bryan Dutt, of Seattle, said they should keep it orange, "just because it's history." I say let's keep Galaxy Gold for the next 50 years!

Abraham
Abei

31

MONORAIL
DRIVER

Getting
ready to depart
from Westlake
Station

Talking with
customers
with all
different
parts of
the work

Working at the monorail is the best
thing I've ever had

They keep the old monorail rolling

Sketched Jan. 23, 2012

The Seattle Center Monorail never became what its creators intended 50 years ago. After the World's Fair, it was meant to be either expanded or dismantled; the concrete columns were bolted to Fifth Avenue so they could be easily removed.

In a way, it was a failed project. But consider the lives touched by the 1.2-mile ride between downtown and Seattle Center. Think of the fun it brings to nearly 2 million tourists every year and to those who commute on it every day. And think of what it means to the people who work there.

For Abraham Abei, David Guet and Joseph Deng, all in their early 30s, the monorail has provided jobs and a path to education — tuition assistance is a perk of working for Seattle Monorail Services. These three are among the thousands of "Lost Boys of Sudan" who escaped the atrocities of their country's civil war in the late '80s. Their reactions to the monorail when they first saw it: "I thought it would fall off," said Deng. And now: "It's the best thing I ever had," said Abei.

Jayme Gustilo, 61, a cashier and a 23-year monorail veteran, said: So what if a ride on the monorail doesn't take you very far; "The journey is more important than the destination."

DANGER
HI-VOLTAGE

Humphre

↑ Bill Humphreys
Monorail technician

1·23·12   11:14 a.m

southern cymbid...
sphe...
elev...

to...

Jin
Jup
11
71
ET

2·10 p.m.
4·24·12
The WORLD's FAIR   Gene
Bubbleator   Achziger

World's Fair Bubbleator has had its ups and downs

Sketched April 24, 2012

Bubble ... what?

The 1962 World's Fair Bubbleator was an ultra-modern, transparent, spheric lift that took 100 people at a time to "The World of Tomorrow," an exhibit of futuristic images inside what is now KeyArena.

It left a lasting impression on visitors and remained a city attraction through the 1970s, when it was part of the Center House, then known as the Food Circus.

But in the '80s, the Bubbleator's magic popped. Des Moines resident Gene Achziger found it in a heap inside a north Lake Union warehouse where it had been put in storage. It was owned by Seattle Children's hospital, but "They didn't know what to do with it," said Achziger, who paid $1,000 for the pieces to build a greenhouse for his home.

We can still travel on the monorail and take in the views from the Space Needle. Wouldn't it be cool to ride the Bubbleator again?

Achziger, 58, said some parts are missing but it would still be great if somebody was willing to bring the space elevator back to life. He actually never got to ride it as a boy because of the long lines at the fair.

Neal
James
23

3/6/2014

Nothing curious about this old shop's success

Sketched March 6, 2014

Shrunken heads from the Amazon. A two-headed lamb. Totem poles carved by local Native Americans. A hat worn by Chief Seattle.

The Ye Olde Curiosity Shop on Pier 54 isn't the tourist trap I expected. It's like a museum that epitomizes the same weird Seattle I love for its Fremont Troll, Archie McPhee or the Pike Place Gum Wall. Founded in the years of the gold rush by Joseph "Daddy" Standley, a shopkeeper with a fascination with curious objects from far-flung cultures, the business has been a staple of the waterfront since 1904 (it was founded in 1899). The mosquito fleet of privately owned ferries that crisscrossed Puget Sound and the steam locomotives that ran by the store are long gone, yet the shop is still owned by Standley's descendants. (That's his great-great-grandson in my sketch, current store manager Neal James.)

Architects dreaming up the post-viaduct waterfront as a giant playground with floating swimming pools and concert venues may want to stop at the Ye Olde Curiosity Shop for further inspiration. The shop underscores the original identity of the waterfront as a place of commerce and global trade, not just entertainment. And isn't it wise to look at the past when you are trying to envision the future?

We make our own Fudge
32 STEPS

Come on in and take a Look

Ye Olde Curiosity Shop

SINCE 1899

3/6/14

SYLVESTER MUMMY

PULL MY GUNARM FOR A LUCKY SOUVENIR COIN

↑ Not a gambling device. dispenses tokens only

2962

1959 GMC
'We call it the Metropolitan'
Bothell and downtown and
Renton and downtown

12·8·'10
9·57 a.m.

Doug
Thomson
'The Scottish
speaking' 51

Remembers high-school
riding Rainier Beach high school

CRANK

Fare
box

Sleigh riding in a vintage bus

Sketched Dec. 8, 2010

Idle buses and trolleys fill row after row at a bus-storage lot in Tukwila, white and brown coaches from the 1940s, bright red GMCs from the '60s and even one of the old waterfront streetcars, barely recognizable under peeling paint. This is where King County's bus fleet comes to die, said Doug Thomson, a 25-year Metro employee. "We call it the boneyard."

But not all of the buses actually die. Since the early '80s, the Metro Employees Historic Vehicle Association has restored more than a dozen and uses them to take people on tours. With more than 400 expected passengers on nine buses, the "Santa's Lights" tour is the most popular of the six they do every year.

Thomson, a light-rail operator by day, enjoys the challenge of maneuvering the old buses through narrow neighborhood streets, calling out the most spectacular lights and singing carols. The best part, he said, is getting into the holiday spirit. "I get to wear my reindeer ears and be one of Santa's helpers."

METROPOLITAN

2962 C 33672

SEATTLE TRANSIT SYSTEM

Doug Thomson

King County's historic buses
12·8·10
11·50 a.m.

The other bridge ↓

1:13 p.m.
2.6.13

A not-so-quiet stroll to Mercer Island

Sketched Feb. 6, 2013

The side-by-side Interstate 90 floating bridges were built for cars and buses, but if you're not in a hurry, I recommend a visit on foot to gain a new perspective on these transportation wonders.

If you start on the pedestrian lane along the north span, you'll recognize the portal over the westbound lanes — that's what you see when you drive into Seattle.

The original art-deco portal is another story. Besides quick glances in the rearview mirror as you drive east, there is little time to appreciate it. Those semicircular tunnels handled traffic in both directions when the bridge opened in 1940. I was able to make a sketch from 35th Avenue South.

Despite the loud traffic, I relished the 50-minute walk to Mercer Island and back. I spotted a great blue heron perched on a buoy, flapping its wings at the wind, took a peek at some waterfront mansions and watched cyclists zoom by.

MOHAI
At old Naval
Reserve.

MOHAI looks truly shipshape

Sketched Jan. 3, 2013

When the Museum of History & Industry moved to the old Naval Reserve Building or armory last month, the art-deco building from the Depression era became its newest, and largest, exhibition piece.

I've seen the monumental building many times, but I had never noticed how much it looks like an actual ship ready to sail into Lake Union.

The design wasn't just a cute idea. Built in 1942, the armory was a training center for the Navy for more than five decades. Inside its "bridge," which faces the lake, Navy reservists sharpened their navigational skills overlooking the water.

That room now features MOHAI's maritime galleries, including a 40-foot submarine periscope that gives visitors a 360-degree view above Lake Union Park.

Lake
Union

MOHAI

1/3/13

NORTH

ART FOR ALL

An artful pole topped with a weather vane is the centerpiece of the Weather Watch Park, a hidden public space built on the site of an ancient ferry dock in West Seattle. Designed by local artist Lezlie Jane, the pole also includes historic photos and fascinating weather facts.

WEATHER WATCH PARK

SW CAROLL ST. AND BEACH DR. SW

A baby and mama Apatosaurus topiary has been a fixture of the Burke-Gilman Trail in Seattle's Fremont neighborhood since the late 1990s, when a group of "Fremonsters" bought the metal structures for $1 and turned them into a piece of public art.

75°

OLYMPIC SCULPTURE PARK

5·13·14

Nov 23 · 2·14 p.m.

snow!

Adel
Espineli
San Diego
with Alana, thinking of J-school

the Fremont
Troll

The Olympic Sculpture Park opened in 2007 on the former site of a fuel-storage facility that took years to clean up. I took advantage of an unusually warm and clear day in May to sketch this view of my favorite artwork there: Alexander Calder's "Eagle."

Thanks to the Fremont Troll, this space under the Aurora Bridge is far from the dumping ground it used to be. Back in 1990, you would find mattresses and beer cans lying around, Steve Badanes told me. Badanes was the lead artist for this project.

8
21
12

Rooftop
P-Patch
MERCER
GARAGE

Communities Come Together

The Seattle area is made up of a tapestry of people, occupations and interests that give the region its unique personality. Sketchbook in hand, I'm always eager to meet the people within each of those unique urban tribes — whether they are fishermen, urban farmers, adventurous scuba divers or aviation enthusiasts.

An old purple Ford Galaxy has been converted into a planting bed at the Mercer Parking Garage P-Patch.
Urban gardener Craig Moore said it is a "good reminder of what was here before."

FRUIT BAGS
Milton
Tam
67
North
side
2.5
acres.
This
will
be the
First
year
that
it's
all
Season
Rotate

You can't spell P-Patch without Picardo

Sketched March 13, 2013

I t has nothing to do with peas.
The P in P-Patch comes from the Picardos, the family of Italian immigrants who farmed the land in Wedgwood where Seattle's first community garden was established in 1973.

"This is a unique Seattle term," said Milton Tam, a gardener who coordinates the 2-acre site and the nearly 600 fellow volunteers eager to see spring coming around.

The Picardo Patch is a remnant of the neighborhood's semirural past, when it was outside the city limits. Since the 1920s, family patriarch Ernesto Picardo grew vegetables to sell in Seattle, but after he died in 1961, the land sat unused for years. Eventually, with permission from the family, neighbors began farming a portion of the fertile soil, which the city purchased to preserve the community-gardening experience. Thus, Seattle's original P-Patch was born.

Forty years later, an urban-gardening movement seems well-rooted in the city. You could say that the P in P-Patch also stands for something else: popular. Just to get one of the estimated 270 plots at Picardo's, people have to wait "six months to a year," said Tam.

Check out (really) these tools

Sketched Dec. 19 and 27, 2012

The shelves are filled with circular saws, power drills and more types of hammers than I ever knew existed. But this is no hardware store. I'm in North Ravenna at the city's newest tool library, where members will be able to check out tools for free after it opens Jan. 19.

The grass-roots project led by Susan Gregory makes a lot of sense. Everyone may own a hammer, she said, but most of us don't need to own expensive tools that we seldom use, such as a shop vacuum or a chain saw.

Modeled after a similar initiative in West Seattle, the NE Seattle Tool Library has already collected more than 600 donated tools.

Tool library member Morgan Redfield, for example, donated a drill press that belonged to his dad, who passed away last year. He "would be really happy if he knew his tools are being used by other people," Redfield told me while I sketched him.

You'll find the NE Seattle Tool Library in a humble building at 2415 N.E. 80th St.

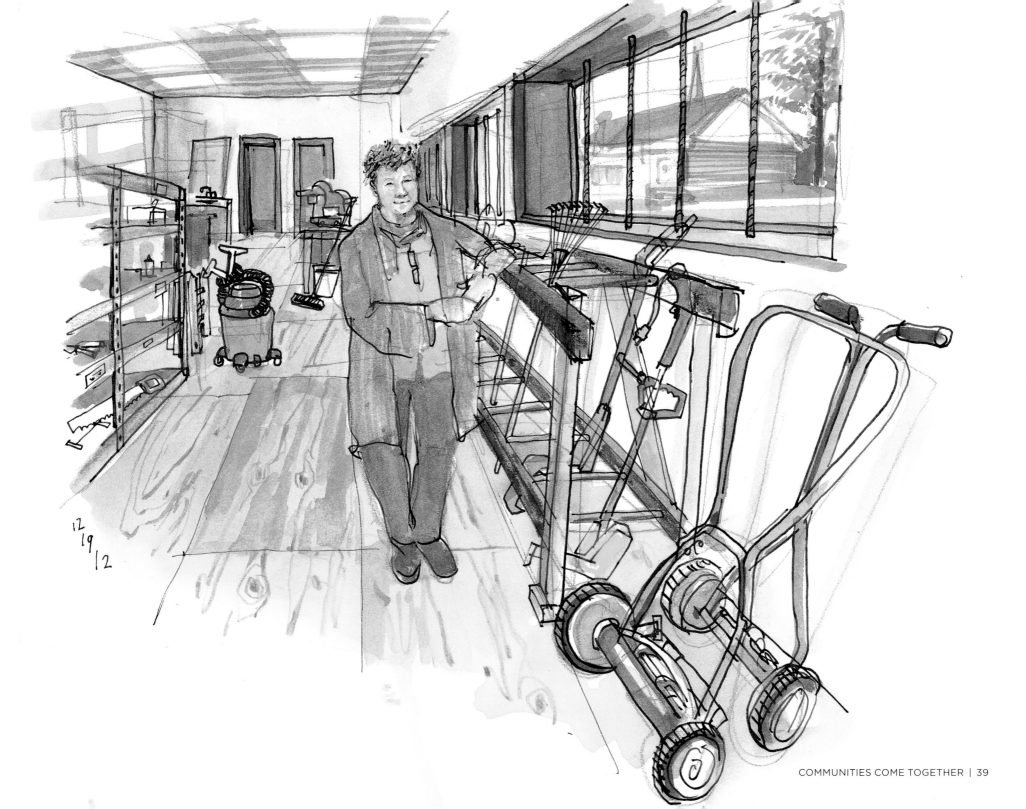

12
19
12

Lisa Sheffield
and her Bourbon Red turkeys

35

Fun to watch
and watch them poo

Bourbon county, Kentucky

11·11·11
11·18 a.m.

For backyard-farm family, a rare bird

Sketched Nov. 11, 2011

Seven months ago, Lisa Sheffield's turkeys were so little her 2½-year-old could hold them in his hands. Now they are nearly 15 pounds each, and although they'll survive this Thanksgiving, Sheffield plans to serve them on the family's dinner table before the end of the year.

Sheffield, a biologist from Oregon who moved into her Northgate home two years ago, doesn't know anyone else in Seattle raising backyard turkeys for meat. She said urban farmers are more likely to raise chickens for eggs and as pets. Turkeys may not have caught on, she added, because they need more space and bark like dogs. They also peck at sketchbooks, I learned.

Sheffield and her husband, Troy Guy, also a biologist, believe in a sustainable backyard economy, and that it's important for their son, Miles, to grow up knowing where food comes from.

Little Miles, who also enjoys playing with the family's seven chickens, has learned the lesson. "Turkeys … we eat them all up."

VP GARDEN
P-PATCH ON MERCER
GARAGE ROOFTOP
7.05 P.M.

Gardeners savor season atop Mercer Street Garage

Sketched Aug. 21, 2012

The Mercer Street Garage rooftop P-Patch, which opened in early June, is starting to yield some crops.

I tasted a tomatillo from Stephanie Krimmel and Craig Moore's plot and it was pretty sweet. Who knew you could garden in a few feet of soil laid over concrete?

To help build the P-Patch, the Krimmel-Moore family put in 150 hours of labor — the most of all volunteers vying for a plot. That gave them first choice of the 98, 100-square-foot plots available. They picked one with great views of the garden's terraces, not to mention the city skyline and the soaring Space Needle.

Being up here, you forget where you are, said Krimmel. "You barely see the cars. You barely hear the street. You are in your own little oasis."

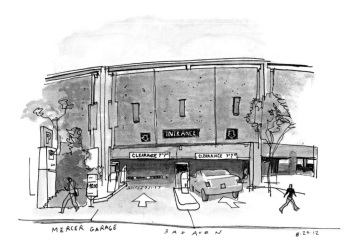

MERCER GARAGE   3RD AVEN   8-29-12

← Mc Caw Hall

8/21/12
1:41
p.m.

URban
gardening
by the
Space Needle

CRAig
MOORE
43

This is →
the
tomatillo I ate!

Sketching on the fly while in the sky

Sketched May 8, 2013

"Are you thinking of flying today?"

When Marc Chirico asked the question, I mumbled: "Er … I wasn't planning to."

Chirico, who runs a paragliding school at the foot of Tiger Mountain in Issaquah, has a long resume in the sport. He has participated in international competitions and once flew 65 miles between Chelan and Odessa in Eastern Washington — a state record.

He also has a knack for making people feel at ease. After watching about a dozen pilots take off, I took up his offer to fly a tandem. Talk about gaining a new perspective!

A burst of wind lifted the featherweight wing and we soared into the sky.

A few minutes later, as the warm air of a thermal propelled us, I pulled out my sketchbook and drew Mount Rainier with my feet dangling in the sky.

"Can you feel the heat?" Chirico asked.

"Oh, yeah."

5·8·2013 MARC CHIRICO
Seattle Paragliding pioneer

Scuba, serenity in Puget Sound

Sketched July 31, 2012

Even on the warmest summer day, swimming in the chilly water of Puget Sound isn't quite as inviting as just looking at it.

If you are admiring the view near the Edmonds ferry dock, though, don't be surprised to see scuba divers pop out of the water. Clad in wet suits, the divers emerge from the Edmonds Underwater Park, a network of submarine trails maintained by volunteers for more than 30 years.

From the shoreline, all you can see are the bright colored buoys that mark the boundaries of the 27-acre park. Under the surface, divers get an up-close look at sea life as they swim through sunken vessels, concrete blocks and tractor tires.

It's a whole different world down there, Jaclyn Perry told me after a 90-minute dive with her buddy. "It's very peaceful. … You can only hear your own bubbles."

Ligh
?
45
low
close
to
100
roow

Jaclyn
PERRY
19

EdMonds
underwater
PARK

7/31/12   4:17
           P.M.

7/31/12

Edmonds Underwater Park

6.02 p.m.

Henry Nelson with his 1940 Cadillac Sedan

Mr. Cliff

Aging well: It's showtime
for old club's old cars

Sketched Aug. 18, 2010

I'm not what you would call a car aficionado, but cars run in my family. My dad was an autoworker for 35 years in Spain and I married the daughter of a retired GM autoworker. I thought of both of them as I sketched members of Old Rides Car Club Seattle, a car club started by Central Area automobile enthusiasts in 1972.

Henry Nelson, who owns a 1940 Cadillac sedan, prides himself on being one of the club's founders. He said Old Rides is the longest-running predominantly African-American car club north of Los Angeles.

Nelson is also a GM retiree like my father-in-law, but not every club member has ties to the industry. Clifford Holland, a former grocery-store manager, is drawn to classic cars because they give him a sense of pride. His 1956 Ford Thunderbird is the model he longed to own when he was 15 but couldn't afford until his mid-30s.

Valerie Pipkin, who owns a 1955 Buick Roadmaster, likes collecting cars for more aesthetic reasons. "They look like rolling pieces of art," she told me as I sketched her masterpiece on wheels.

Valerie Pipkin with her
1955 Buick Roadmaster

HAWK ONE TAILGATE PARTY

At Emerald Queen Casino in Fife, WA

Hawk One is a tailgating Taj Mahal

Sketched Sept. 8, 2013

Talk about team spirit.

Gary Buchanan, Brian Miller and Tony Wetzel don't just root for the Seahawks. They have their own 38-foot tailgating RV to rally fans before games.

The interior of the motor home is a mini-museum of the team's history. The ceiling looks like that of the old Kingdome stadium, and names of legendary Seahawk players are displayed on a "Ring of Honor." There's more Kingdome-era stuff all around: three red chairs from the old stands, a piece of green turf and even a chunk of concrete from the arena demolished 13 years ago.

The custom bar, which stands on legs shaped like goal posts, displays the original Seahawk logo, based on Native American tribal art. The osprey doesn't have the mean eye of the current logo, noted Miller, who is a toolmaker by day and did most of the handiwork inside the vehicle.

Hawk One looks so polished you might think it's an official marketing gimmick. It's not.

"We are the core 12th Man," said Buchanan, who is looking forward to bringing the "ultimate tailgating experience" to "Hawk Alley" for a fifth year in a row Sunday, with the game against the San Francisco 49ers. "A thousand people will show up. It will be crazy."

RING OF HONOR 22 DAVE BROWN 76-85

HAWK ONE

Brian
Miller
co-owner

3

9
8
13

9·8·13
Tailgating inside HawK one,
at Emerald Queen Casino

Big Nations
tailgating championshi

Piece of teel and

Result:
SEAHAWKS
12
PANTHERS
7

it wasn't pretty but
it was a win!

Pier 86 is a little less crowded, a lot more cozy

Sketched July 5, 2011

People come to this long pier at Terminal 86 to catch all sorts of marine life, depending on the time of the year: lingcod, rockfish, Dungeness crab, salmon and squid.

Terry Stroud is one of about a dozen regulars. There's also Ken, Cris, Rich ... When they catch a big fish, they snap a photo and put it up on the "wall of fame" inside the pier's shelter. "We are like a big family down here," said Stroud, who once caught a 29.5-pound lingcod.

They like Pier 86 because it's not as crowded as other fishing spots in the city. At the Spokane Street Bridge in West Seattle, it'll be "elbow to elbow" when salmon arrive in late July. The busiest time at this pier is actually in October and November, Stroud said. People fish for squid at night, and the Happy Hooker Bait & Tackle Shop stays open until midnight.

With lingcod season over, Stroud wasn't expecting to catch anything, much less a 21-armed starfish with a bright-orange golf ball lodged in its mouth. "I told you the water was polluted," said Stroud with a laugh. He used his tweezers to extricate the golf ball and handed it to me. "That's your lucky ball."

21

it looks
better at night
after the sunset
when the lights are on

there's scar

I usually come
in at night
9 - 1a.m
It's really quiet
at night

pier 91
1 cruise ships

Pier 66 → 25 pound ling cod
around one 10
6 years
Beacon Hill

Jeff Zhao , 21

I eat all of them
Rock Fish
they taste
better

7/5/11

Rock Fish
Ling cod

it has a lot of fish

I like sean Fishing with my uncle in China — catfish/tilapia

here I go around — change spots

NE 45th St

Deluxe

SPECIA

CHEESEBURGER

← Ketchup

← Mustard

1/16/14

Matt   ↑   ↑
      on the   wRappeR
      grill

goopers

it's the same
taste

Orange john - diet coke   was
cleaning all the time

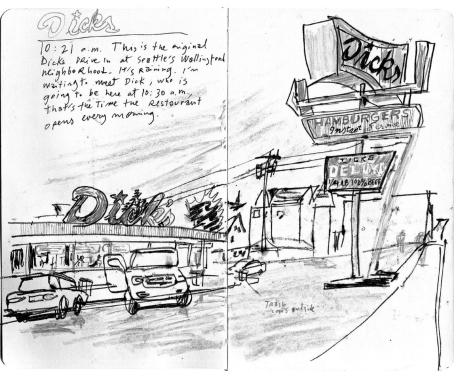

Dick's Drive-In flips simple, beloved burgers

Sketched Nov. 10, 2009, and Jan. 16, 2014

I didn't choose a good weather day for my first visit to Dick's Drive-In, the beloved Seattle eatery founded by Dick Spady in 1954. The rain got my sketchbook all wet, but the occasion was memorable in many ways. I had my first Dick's Deluxe hamburger and met Spady himself — he even autographed my sketch.

My only disappointment was realizing that Dick's burgers don't come with my favorite ingredient: a slice of tomato.

Years later, when I returned to draw inside the kitchen, I discovered that the no-tomato policy doesn't have much to do with tomatoes per se. Adding any extra ingredients would be a huge change, marketing director Jasmine Donovan told me.

She didn't entirely rule out the possibility, but since there have been few menu changes in the history of Dick's — like when orange soda was dropped to make way for Diet Coke — I'm not going to get my hopes up.

JET CITY

During World War II, Velva Maye was one on a four-woman team in charge of ordering the rivets, clamps, nuts and bolts that kept Boeing's famed "Flying Fortresses" together. After retiring with 40 years of service, she and other volunteers helped restore a B-17F that is now part of the Museum of Flight collection.

Angel Flight West
Seattle → Albany, ORe.

Bob Schaper

Ed Bryce

Sierra Lorenzo
18
5.30.13

Bob Schaper is one of about 90 pilots in Western Washington who fly humanitarian missions for Angel Flight West. He takes patients to doctor appointments and delivers donated blood to a Puget Sound Blood Center collection point at Boeing Field.

Retired Boeing employee Terry "TC" Howard, a volunteer at the Museum of Flight Restoration Center in Everett, showed me the first 727 jetliner to roll off the Boeing assembly line. It's parked not far from the runway at Paine Field where it landed for the first time in 1963 after taking off from Boeing Field.

TC Howard

lightblu

UNITED

7001

"First 727 out of the Assembly Line."

Just Landing

← Forklift

KENMORE AIRPORT
2.40 p.m.

Personnel at Kenmore Air Harbor Marina on the north shore of Lake Washington use forklifts to move the seaplanes in and out of the water. Kenmore Air, known for its service to the San Juan Islands and British Columbia, is the largest seaplane operator in the U.S.

28th AVE NE

The Wedgwood Rock

4·15·14

Secret Spots Revealed

Reader tips of unique places in the Seattle area are always music to my ears. How else would I have ever found a lake surrounded by so many houses you can't even see the water from the street? Or a national park housed inside a downtown building? My Seattle roots grow deeper the more I know what only locals know.

Local mountaineers used this "erratic boulder" to practice their rock-climbing skills decades ago, before the city enforced a climbing ban in 1970.

9/9/10

Queen Anne

West
Lake
Union
Floating
homes

"Sleepless" house keeps drawing attention

Sketched Sept. 8, 2010

More than a decade after "Sleepless in Seattle" romanticized houseboat living, curious tourists still sneak into Lake Union docks searching for the home of Sam Baldwin, the sleepless widower played by Tom Hanks in the 1993 blockbuster.

I felt a bit like one of the tourists when I visited Eugene Nutt and Ann Bassetti at the houseboat where they've lived since 1988. From their living room, they had a front-row seat for the making of the movie. They recalled holiday decorations and a "big crane with a massive shower head" to produce rain in August.

There are only about 500 floating homes now, down from a couple of thousand in the 1930s, so I'm not surprised this unique community is such an attraction.

The tours offered by the Floating Homes Association every two years sell out pretty fast.

HALLER
LAKE

DOGS
NOT...

5/16/12 3:
15
p.m.

chica

Seattle's most hidden lake

Sketched May 16, 2012

I drove and walked around this small lake in North Seattle several times before finally finding the slice of shoreline that is open to the public.

Haller Lake is certainly a hidden lake, and for those who are lucky enough to live around it, a true oasis of nature in the middle of the city.

I was almost done with my sketch when Devona Hutsell approached me with her Chihuahua, Chica, and asked me to add her to my drawing. The result turned out to be rather "grande" in scale compared to the rest of the scene, but Hutsell seemed pleased. She said this lake is a well-kept secret. "The only people who know it are the people who grew up here."

Another well-hidden gem in this neighborhood is the Haller Lake Community Club. Members of the Puget Sound Theatre Organ Society come here for "Pizza and Pipes." They unbox a historic Wurlitzer pipe organ and delight audiences with pizza, show tunes and silent-movie comedies.

Where Tully's Coffee broke fresh grounds

Sketched Jan. 30, 2013

Most people know the first Starbucks is at Pike Place Market. But how about the first Tully's? Company founder Tom Tully O'Keefe told me it was in a shopping center near Panther Lake in Kent, but it has been closed for more than a decade.

As far as he remembered, the next Tully's Coffee shops opened in Mercer Island, Clyde Hill and Capitol Hill soon after in the early '90s. The one in Clyde Hill, a city on the Eastside I had yet to visit, used to be his home store when he lived in Medina.

Here coffee-shop manager Joel Pearson has fixed drinks for the likes of Steve Ballmer and the Gates family. That's nothing to be surprised about, he said, given that Clyde Hill and the surrounding communities of Yarrow Point, Hunts Point and Medina rank at the top in the state based on per capita income.

Because of its location right off Highway 520, this Tully's has also become a convenient destination for Seattle and Eastside professionals to meet, said Pearson, who guessed the number of people who spread out on the tables with their laptops is in the "hundreds per week."

Tully's, clyde Hill

'30
'13

Historical photos

Park
Ranger
Tim J.
Karle

Klondike
Gold Rush
National Park
SEATTLE

Klondike Gold Rush NHP
JUN 20 2013
Seattle, WA

it was a matter of luck

"Few people ever saw gold on their pans"
"It was a matter of luck"

Pioneer Square's indoor national park

Sketched June 20 and 26, 2013

All this time I've thought the closest national parks to Seattle were Mount Rainier, the North Cascades and the Olympics. But here's one that is even closer: the Klondike Gold Rush National Historical Park in Pioneer Square.

Veteran park ranger Tim J. Karle said I'm not the only visitor who is surprised when stepping into the building. People expect trees and mountains, he said. Instead, they find themselves wandering through two floors of exhibits.

I'm more of an urban hiker than an outdoors explorer anyway, so I wasn't at all disappointed. I enjoyed the 23-minute movie "Gold Fever: Rush to the Klondike" and watching Karle's demonstration of gold-panning techniques.

The park gave me a better understanding of Seattle's history and its entrepreneurial spirit. Most stampeders who came through town on their way to the Klondike River never saw gold on their pans, said Karle, but they helped launch Seattle as the gateway to Alaska. These days, "Tourism is the modern gold rush."

WEST
SEATTLE BRIDGE

METRO BUS

2.33 p.m.
5·18·11
TERMINAL
1B Public Access Park

In memory
of LEE E. FLICK
[For his untiring efforts
to make HARBOR Island
a better place to WORK
and do business]

Port decked with "hidden gems"

Sketched May 18, 2011

They call them "hidden gems" for a reason. The 20-plus parks maintained by the Port of Seattle near its facilities are not easy to find. Some have names like Terminal 18 Park or Terminal 105 Park, so don't bet on Google Maps to get you there. But don't be discouraged. Once you get past the railroad tracks, dirt roads and chain-link fences, you'll relish the discovery.

At Jack Block Park, one of the few that would show up on my iPhone map search, I couldn't believe my luck. An observation deck 45 feet above the shoreline offers the closest view of the city skyline from West Seattle. You can also see container terminals and hear seals from a 250-foot-long boardwalk.

Hank Fridal, out with his Boston terriers, said Jack Block is perfect to bring guests from out of town. They are amazed, he said. "Living so close to this, you can't ever have a bad day."

JACK BLOCK PARK

Smith Tower

Safeco field

WATER TAXI

5/18/2011

12 38 p.m.

3 poun
TO
10
poun

THeRe's
a King
here
too,
I've
seen
a Few

PAt
MARtinez,
FisheRman

The little
one
are
King
up
To
45
pounds

come
here
in two
or three
weeks,
these
windows
will be
Full
to

It's
a
was
trip

I'm
a Fishem
I came
here to
see
what's
coming
up
Hopefully

6/16/10

9:05
a.m.

A room with a view of fish

Sketched June 16, 2010

From kayaks to luxury yachts and fishing boats, the steady flow of vessels at the Hiram M. Chittenden Locks is enough to keep a guy like me entertained. They go by so close you can even strike up a conversation. "We are going out for a month," said a boater on her way to the Sound.

Another spectacle is found below the water level at the fish ladder. I would have never been able to tell what type of salmon I was looking at, but it was my luck to run into Pat Martinez, a local fisherman who makes a quick stop every day to check the activity on the ladder.

Martinez said these were all sockeye, except for a few king salmon, which looked much larger. "Sockeyes can be from 3 to 10 pounds," he said. "King salmon can go up to 45 pounds."

I love that someone had the vision to create the fish ladder when the locks were built in the 1910s. Without it, the salmon's life cycle would have been completely disrupted. I also appreciate that when they rebuilt it in 1976 they added this viewing area where I sketched. It makes for a great educational experience.

DAVID BERGER

MOUNT
BAKER
RIDGE VIEWPOINT

6 12 13

6/12/13

↑SUMMER SOLSTICE SUNSET MARKER — MOUNT BAKER Ridge Viewpoint.

Mount Baker viewpoint lets you find your place in the universe

Sketched June 12, 2013

I've yet to visit a Seattle location that says so much about our longing for sun as the Mount Baker Ridge Viewpoint.

The pocket park perched on a slope directly above the Interstate 90 tunnel is a contemporary "Stonehenge" where you can track the star moving through the seasons. Seven basalt stones that could be mistaken as places to sit align with the horizon points where the sun sets at different times of the year, including the solstices and the equinoxes.

I visited hoping to see the last rays of daylight shine through the notch on the summer-solstice stone, but you can guess what prevented me from sketching that: a big cloud!

David Berger, who led the community effort to create the park, said the fascination with the sun isn't just a Seattle thing. It's common to many cultures, and it may have something to do with "finding our place in the universe."

Leif
Erikson

Ancestor
of all who
emigrated
from Nordic
Lands

Shilshole
Marina

7/25/12

12·12 p.m.

"Our boy Leif" standing tall at Shilshole Marina

Sketched July 25, 2012

The statue of Leif Erikson at Shilshole Marina had a rough start back in the 1960s. When local Scandinavians offered it to the city, some government art officials deemed it "unexciting." But the Port of Seattle had the wisdom to accept the gift, which has been a fixture of the marina for decades.

Kristine Leander, of the Leif Erikson International Foundation, agrees that the 17-foot sculpture looks a bit like "a football player with a Viking helmet." But its artistic value is not the point.

To Scandinavian Americans, she said, "our boy Leif" represents risk-taking immigrants who came with their "sails filled with hope and courage."

Leif's statue has been part of a new plaza at the marina since its rededication in 2007. Surrounding stones display the names of more than 1,700 Scandinavian immigrants and benches invite a moment of contemplation. Leander said it's become almost a spiritual place.

A lesser-known landmark of the marina is Shilly the Sea Monster. It rises above the breakwater barrier following its spooky guardian.

SHilshole MARiNA   7·25·2012
"shilly the seamonster"

5°
2
57
p.m.

CONVENTION CENTER

Anny

Antonio

Olivia

Yuri

Nick
Klacsanzky

Meditation
at Freeway
Park

Shoes

8/11/10

12:29 p.m.

Au
SAR
Ou
A

Serenity in the city's chaos

Sketched Aug. 11, 2010

If you haven't been to Freeway Park, you may think I just made this sketch up. What's this forest surrounded by skyscrapers? And that cascading waterfall?

This labyrinth of concrete and greenery straddling Interstate 5 connects First Hill and downtown. I usually drive under it, but this morning I took a walk through it for the first time, starting at Paul Pigott Memorial Corridor at Ninth Avenue and University Street.

Neighbor Joan Carufel had the perfect description for what I was seeing. "This is an oasis," she said. "It's the breathing space for downtown Seattle."

It was under the shade of the park's trees that I sketched a group of people attending a meditation class, a scene I would have never expected to find at a park so close to a noisy highway.

Meditation instructor Nick Klacsanzky said he didn't mind the roaring of cars zooming by on I-5. "You can find serenity in the middle of the chaos of the city," he said. "If you can find peace inside, you can meditate anywhere."

ALKI
POINT
LIGHTHOUSE
8·8·13

Shedding light on a familiar beacon

Sketched Aug. 8, 2013

Perfect timing. The morning low tide allowed me to walk far out on the beach south of Alki Point and find a good angle to sketch Seattle's most-hidden lighthouse.

Boaters may be very familiar with the beacon that marks the southern entrance to Elliott Bay (Did you know it flashes every five seconds?). But for those of us spending all our time on dry land, it's not easy to get a close look.

First, there are the beach houses surrounding the historic landmark, which turned 100 this summer. Though I was able to walk around them at low tide, I couldn't help but feel I was sneaking into somebody's backyard.

Second, the lighthouse complex is an active Coast Guard station that houses the residence of the commander of the 13th Coast Guard District. Walk by the entrance on Alki Avenue Southwest, and you realize this is not your typical tourist attraction.

But it's still possible to visit the lighthouse. During the summers or by appointment, Coast Guard volunteers give free tours of the complex.

12.21 p.m.   ALKI POINT LIGHTHOUSE

B. B. 13

66°

CITY OF BOATS

The Smith Cove Cruise Terminal on the Magnolia waterfront has been the home port for Alaska-bound cruises since 2009. The cruise ships are so huge, even large boats like the Victoria Clipper ferry look tiny in comparison.

PIER 91

people

The Victoria Clipper

Carnival Spirit, departing in just an hour or so.
3:11 p.m
July 13, 2010

Within the illustration:
11 26 13
LTJG PAUL GARCIA
POLAR STAR
icebreaker
Preparing to sail to Antarctica in a few days.

Few other Seattle-based ships capture my imagination like the U.S. Coast Guard icebreakers at Pier 36. Deck officer Paul Garcia told me they are the only vessels that can reach the polar ice caps by their own means, able to cut through blocks of ice two-stories high.

Western Towboats crew getting
ready to sail to Whittier, Alaska

western navigator   Western Ranger

The family-owned Western Towboat Co., based in Ballard, has been in the business of maritime transportation of goods since 1948. It has a fleet of 21 tugs and about 140 employees.

1·11·11
8:38
a.m.
West Seattle
Water Taxi
at Seacrest
Park dock

The word taxi doesn't do justice to the service provided by the West Seattle Water Taxi, a vessel connecting the downtown waterfront and West Seattle. Water bus seems more fitting for a scheduled ferry that carries up to 150 people.

12.58
p.m   10·26·11
viaduct demolition

Changing Landscapes

An architect once told me that every neighborhood has hidden clues that help create a sense of belonging for the people. As an urban sketcher, I relish finding those still-standing signs of history, such as an old house surrounded by shiny new buildings or an ancient warehouse reused as a fashionable furniture showroom.

The sheer magnitude of the demolition of a segment of the Alaskan Way Viaduct in Sodo created an interested scene. "It's gorgeous ... in an odd sort of way," said one of the onlookers.

owen
with
his
dog

aqua

4.40 p.m.

← rai tnu

Arizona
folks lost looking for 'open air market

owned by Owen Millette
carpenter
viaduct - This is crazy and this thing is crowded

A day under the viaduct

Sketched Aug. 30, 2011

"**A**n elevated freeway right on the waterfront? What a waste of space."

That's what my little tourist brain thought about the Alaskan Way Viaduct when I first visited Seattle in 1995, more than a decade before I moved here for good.

But now I understand why the viaduct is there. When it was built in 1953, the waterfront wasn't quite the playground for tourists it is today. It was a logical spot to build the city's first major transportation corridor, replacing some of the railroad tracks that had run along the industrial shoreline since the late 1800s.

During a recent walk under the aging freeway, I met day laborers, lost tourists looking for Pike Place Market, ferry commuters, the homeless and entrepreneurs who set up their businesses here decades ago. Most of them agreed there's not much they'll miss about the viaduct itself when it is all demolished in a few years. Not the noise, not the obstructed views.

Ken Eubank, who opened his Seattle Antique Market in the shadow of the viaduct in 1978, fears small businesses may not survive the redevelopment of the waterfront. But they won't miss the threat of the freeway falling down during an earthquake. He recalled seeing streetlights along the top swinging back and forth like fishing poles when the 6.8-magnitude Nisqually quake hit in 2001.

Ken Eubank

1130

3:41 p.m.

Troy Laundry won't be completely washed away by development

Sketched Jan. 6, 2012, and July 8, 2014

I've had my eye on the Troy Laundry building in South Lake Union since I started working at The Seattle Times, which is just around the corner, almost eight years ago.

I used to sketch it from my window at the old Times building. And I've often walked by on my way to lunch or to check the food trucks that congregate in the area. Back in the day, before most people had a washer and dryer at home, the Troy Laundry Co. ran a pretty large operation here. Its fleet of 50 trucks hauled bundles of laundry and dry cleaning from customers as far away as Kirkland and Renton.

Now the 1927 building — owned by The Seattle Times from 1985 to 2011 — is just a shell of itself. Bulldozers have started leveling the block and construction of two high-rise office towers will begin soon.

But I have no reason to be nostalgic. The hollowed-out walls of the historic landmark are being preserved and integrated into the new complex. When the towers are completed, these ornate brick and terra-cotta detailings will provide an interesting juxtaposition of old and new, present and past, not to mention another excuse to leave the office and make more sketches of the rapidly changing neighborhood.

That's AMAZON thru the window

TROY LAUNDRY
built 1927

AMAZON

VE STREET

FAIRVIEW
AVEN.

THOMAS ST.

JANUARY 6, 2012
4.08 p.m.

Last day before move to the Seattle
Times consolidated offices on Denny WAY.
Goodbye view from my old desk!

Handwritten note on left sketch:
FUN FOREST RIDES
March 31, 10:49 a.m.
FOR SALE!

People like to come out when the weather is nice.

Julia King came today from Bainbridge Island.

Handwritten note on right sketch:
11:33 a.m.
1.25.12
View of Chihuly Garden & Exhibit from Space Needle's Skyline Level

Museum rises out of the forest

Sketched March 31, 2010; Jan. 25 and May 8, 2012

From Fun Forest to Glass Garden.

It has been interesting to watch the transformation of the grounds west of the Space Needle since the beloved amusement park closed for good after Labor Day 2010.

The new glass museum devoted to Dale Chihuly's work adds an exuberant touch of color to a city that can often feel so gray.

As an artist, I can imagine how much this might mean to him. What an amazing opportunity to have a permanent exhibit at Seattle Center — the city's living room, as some describe it. Visitors get a full retrospective of Chihuly's career, culminating in a 100-foot-long assemblage of 1,400 glass pieces suspended from the ceiling of the garden's centerpiece "glass house."

The shiny artwork, however, hasn't erased my memories of the Fun Forest yet. Although the rides felt outdated when I first saw them, they still made a big impression on my kids. It was the first time my son drove a bumper car and my daughter had a blast spinning around the Snow Convoy track.

CHIHULY GARDEN AND GLASS

EMP

5-8-12 3:51pm

Edith
Macefield's
House

1438 NW 46th St

SITE
TION

10
16
12

A new purpose for "Edith's House"

Sketched Oct. 16, 2012

The door of the gutted house was cracked open, but I didn't see Edith Macefield's ghost roaming around.

You may remember her story. When Macefield died at age 86 in 2008, a five-story retail and commercial center was being built around her little Ballard house. Despite a $1 million offer from developers, she refused to sell, reminding us with her defiance that some things in life are, well, priceless.

In her will, Macefield left the house to one of the workers she befriended during the construction of the Ballard Blocks. He later sold it for $310,000 to Greg Pinneo, a real-estate investor who announced plans to elevate it 30-feet off the ground and create a space below known as "Credo Square."

Pinneo's business partner Lois MacKenzie said the upgrade is about to begin, though the house won't be elevated. The revised plan is to transform what remains of the tiny cottage into a cozy nightly rental with room for six people, and it may be called "Edith's House at Credo Square."

ITNESS

10 9 12

Edith Macefield's house   1438 NW 46th St

11.27
a.m.
3.6.12

ALFARETTA

PROPOSED LAI

802 SENECA ST

Messy end for First Hill old-timer

Sketched March 6, 2012

The ghostly doorway of the half-demolished Alfaretta Apartments hides the massive ruins of what used to be a typical building on First Hill, a five-story apartment house built in 1918.

How did it come to this? Neighbors told me plans to build condos fell through during the 2008 financial crisis and demolition came to a halt.

Now work may resume with the construction of a proposed 31-story high-rise that would become the tallest building to date on First Hill and among the tallest residential towers in the city. The project would clear the Seneca Street eyesore, add a new access to the adjacent Freeway Park and bring more density to quiet "Pill Hill," but it worries some neighbors, who say a 300-foot tower is of out of scale for the neighborhood.

Early First Hill residents who lived to see five-story buildings like the Alfaretta dwarf their mansions probably felt the same way. The Stimson-Green Mansion is one of a handful of those residences that has survived to stand amid the high-rises.

FIRST HILL   STIMSON-GREEN MANSION   3.6.12

Old soul of Sodo shines out

Sketched Feb. 14, 2012

Ugly Sodo? Mike Peringer didn't like that passing reference from one of my earlier columns. No surprise, as he is the president of the Sodo Business Association and proud of what's going on in his part of town, including the prospect of a new NBA arena.

Peringer said Sodo has been transforming for a few years, with more retail and commercial enterprises altering the once-industrial landscape. A trapeze-arts company now occupies a warehouse where boiler plates were made. On First Avenue South, restored buildings from the 1920s have become event halls and home-improvement stores.

One of those stores occupies this 1918 warehouse across from the Starbucks headquarters. Eight years ago, the charming old woodshed was on the verge of demolition, as it stood on the path of a monorail line that voters eventually rejected. Looking past its tacky signage, I realized these few remaining old buildings are where Sodo's soul and beauty lie.

All that is New

That's part of the movement ↓

Hope! ↓

RAINIER AVE.

That's kind of crazy to see the letters falling out.

The pain of neighborhood change reflected in the lyrics of hip-hop artist Draze

Sketched Feb. 27, 2014

Every time I go to South Seattle and the Central District, I see more and more homes being renovated and new apartment buildings under construction. This city changes fast.

But homegrown hip-hop artist Dumi Maraire, best known as Draze, sees something my eyes have missed: The forces of gentrification are uprooting the black community. "These used to be all black families and black-owned businesses," Draze told me as I sketched him on the steps of his childhood home on South Orcas Street. "Nobody is here anymore."

Including Draze, who now lives in more affordable Renton. I reached out to him after I stumbled upon a video of his most recent song, "The Hood Ain't the Same," on YouTube.

Draze's lyrics mention many black-owned businesses that no longer exist. What once was Sammie's burgers on East Union Street is boarded up and covered with graffiti. The Silver Fork restaurant on Rainier Avenue South closed the day after he brought his crew to shoot the video last summer.

As he drove me around his old haunts in Rainier Valley and the CD, Draze shared his view of gentrification as eloquently as he does in his rap song: "The city is thriving," he said, "but my community is dying. That doesn't feel good."

26th AVE

E UNION ST.

4240

2
27
14

DRAZE says The Hood ain't the same!   LOOKOUT

I got
my
own
room
I couldn't the
4 b
2 b

Trees   "I think
in   we were this"
front   Party
         meeting
         point

This
we built dreams
here

I know they're sounds
really in Kent...
                  - all this
Talk about
OUR music   very low income people   we m
              There are no white   all
                                            blac
                  herding people like cattle....
Boomboxes   it will never be OK not owning this   This was like a hub in the community ll   all types of feelis,   all kid
Hip hop Freestyling Right here on the steps. Rap battles.   From tration   gentrification   mainly people.   Knew
                                              burst   People all our   each
Anger about the   need selfishness.   peer   Regret (Hope)   CARS all the way   other
    situation   it doesn't truly care   power   FeaR   So I can   This is whre l,
It's a mindset that doesn't   I regret my people not putting a stake privilege   When this music goes uck
                                 in the ground ll   It was green and mit   I am going to buy this hse

GAS WORKS PARK

3
40
pm
8
10
11

graffiti
is 2
daysold

New
paint

AURORA
bridge

Happy colors back in play

Sketched Aug. 10, 2011

The labyrinth of steel pipes and boiler towers in the Gas Works Park play barn is getting a colorful facelift.

Originally a compressor room when the plant operated from 1906 to 1956, the space became a brightly painted play area when the park opened in 1975. "It was a real transformation of a grim industrial facility into a real children's play area with a carnival-type atmosphere," said Patrick Waddell, a member of Friends of Gas Works Park.

Over time, layers of graffiti and patches of mismatching paint muddied the fun palette, but last month Waddell's group persuaded the city to restore the Dr. Seussical colors.

Parks Department paint-crew chief Chris Reed said graffiti here is painted over every year before the Fourth of July — some of the main structures just got a fresh coat of brown in June — but this is the first end-to-end paint job in the barn since 1985.

For park visitor Amy Coughlin, 33, the change brings back memories of playing here as a kid. "It's pretty awesome," she said.

8/10/11

2.29 pm

GAS WORKS
PARK
play barn

BUS

GREYHOUND

GREYHOUND
BUS STATION

9·26·13

End of the line for old bus station

Sketched Sept. 26, 2013

The days of the downtown Greyhound bus terminal are numbered. The entire city block where one of Seattle's oldest transportation hubs has stood since 1927 is slated for redevelopment next year. Will we miss it?

The significance of the building may be lost at first sight. The majority of the original brick work was covered with beige ceramic tiles in the 1960s. (What were they thinking?) Mismatched additions like a roof overhang covering the passenger-loading area also mask the integrity of the station.

But consider the history. Decades before buses and light rail shared the downtown bus tunnel, streetcars and buses ran alongside the same wall where I recently sketched passengers boarding the 2:10 p.m. Greyhound to Vancouver, B.C.; part of the rails can still be seen through the pavement.

The Central Stage Terminal, as it was called then, was the southern base of the Seattle-Everett Interurban rail line and home to a number of coach companies that later displaced the streetcars and preceded Greyhound. Call it the first hybrid bus-rail station in the city.

While Greyhound plans to build a new terminal near the Stadium light-rail station early next year, the redevelopment of this site into a massive hotel/residential complex will erase an important part of Seattle's transportation past. The city didn't deem the terminal worthy of landmark status, so don't expect the bulldozers to leave any part of it standing.

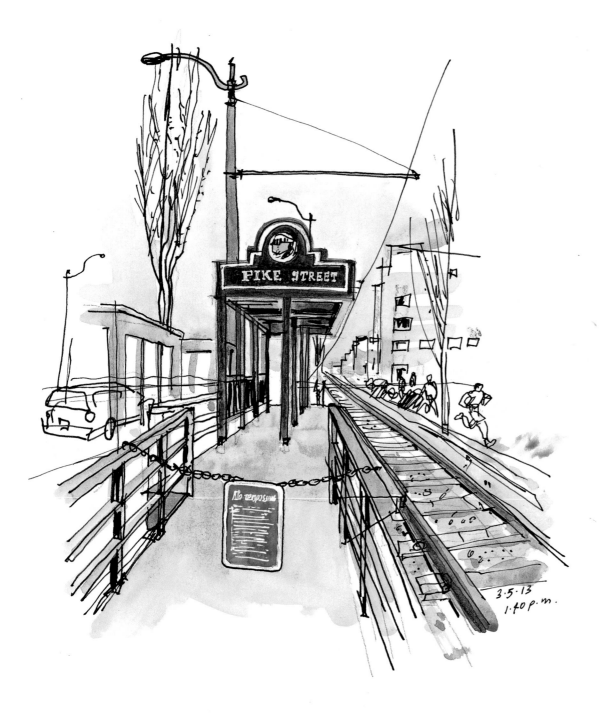

3.5.13
1.40 p.m.

Can old waterfront streetcars get back on track?

Sketched Feb. 27 and March 5, 2013

I've yet to talk to a person in Seattle who didn't love the George Benson waterfront streetcars.

Since 2005, they've been stored at a facility in Sodo where Metro kindly let this newspaper artist roam around.

As I was sizing up the cavernous room, I stumbled upon a "RIDER ALERT" sign still glued to a streetcar door. Talk about a blast from the past: "Beginning Saturday, Nov. 19, the Waterfront Streetcar will be temporarily replaced by Route 99 bus service, pending construction of a new streetcar-maintenance facility."

Why that new facility was never built seems beyond the point now that eight years have passed. My question is: "Will I ever ride one of these?"

Streetcar advocate Tom Gibbs, a retired transit executive, is optimistic. He said the 1.6-mile line that first opened in 1982 could be linked to the First Hill line, which is scheduled to open early next year. And a barn for the new streetcar line planned at Eighth Avenue South and South Dearborn Street could also be expanded to accommodate the beloved trolleys.

Since Metro considered selling them last year, 966 people have signed an online petition at saveourstreetcar. org to restore the legacy of the late City Council member George Benson. Gibbs assured me there is a lot of support out there.

I hope he is right.

482 512 605

2
21
13

548 518 572

GOOD SPORTS

The Mariner Moose poses for photos with fans at Seattle's Safeco Field. The mascot isn't free to roam around the ballpark as I thought. "He has a busy schedule," said Ashley Petersen, the "navigator" assigned to him for this game.

next 5O

LET'S GO STORM

STORM Vs. MYSTICS at KEY ARENA

6·24·12

players returning to the cord

Final score STORM 72 - mystics 55

Going to see the Seattle Storm, two-time WNBA champions, play at KeyArena was a treat for my sports-loving son and a bit of a milestone for me. I had never been to a professional basketball game before.

The most die-hard Sounders FC fans, the Emerald City Supporters, take the bleachers at the south end of Qwest Field and chant for the game's entire 90 minutes. It's a choreographed performance as riveting to watch as an actual game.

On a freezing February day, thousands of parents left work and pulled their kids from school for a glimpse of the Seattle Seahawks. The Hawks brought home the team's first Super Bowl title.

Gabriel Campanario has been a familiar face to readers of The Seattle Times since his sketches started running in the newspaper in 2009. A native of Spain, he began his journalism career in his hometown of Barcelona in the early '90s and joined The Seattle Times' staff in 2006 after stints as a graphic artist and designer for newspapers on both sides of the Atlantic, including USA TODAY, The (Palm Springs, Calif.) Desert Sun and La Vanguardia (Barcelona). Campanario's best-selling book, "The Art of Urban Sketching," was published in 2012 by Quarry Books, and a five-month exhibit of his work took place at the Seattle Museum of History & Industry in 2014. He lives in the Seattle area with his wife and two children, and never leaves home without a sketchbook in his pocket.

A sunset view of the Olympic Mountains from the Water Tower in Volunteer Park.